McGraw Hill Companies
2460 Kerper Blvd.
Dubuque, Iowa 52001

THE ALLEN-BRADLEY

SLC™ 50/1-2

PROGRAMMABLE CONTROLLER

A Programmed Text/Lab Manual

Developed By

Archie Campbell, Master Instructor

The McGraw-Hill Companies, Inc
Primis Custom Publishing
*New York St. Louis San Francisco Auckland Bogota
Caracas Lisbon London Madrid Mexico Milan Montreal
New Delhi Paris San Juan Singapore Sydney Tokyo Toronto*

McGraw-Hill

A Division of The McGraw-Hill Companies

7 8 9 0   QPD   0

ISBN 0-07-232766-9

Table of Contents

Unit 1 ....Overview of the SLC™ 50/1 Programmable Controller.............................1-1

Modules used with Demo Box 1-1

Demo Box Loads and Switches...1-3

The Hand Held Terminal (HHT)..1-4

Example of Ladder Diagram 1-5

Preliminary Steps Prior to Applying Power to the Programmable Logic Controller...........1-5

Applying Power to The PLC 1-5

Familiarization with the HHT..1-6

Unit 2 ....Configuring the Controller 2-7

Controller Configuration Steps..2-7

Self-Test 2-9

Unit 3 ....Naming the Program File..3-11

Unit 4 ....Memory Organization and Addressing..4-13

Program Files 4-13

Data Files..4-14

Addressing the Files..4-14

Self-Test 4-17

Unit 5 ....Entering, Saving, and Running a One...5-19

Rung Program..5-19

Entering a One Rung Program..5-19

Saving a Program 5-20

Running the Program 5-20

Clearing the CPU and HHT 5-21

Unit 6 .... Modifying a Rung **6-23**

Changing Addresses with the ZOOM Control 6-25

Making Changes to Rungs 6-26

Unit 7 .... Entering a Multi-Rung Program Using the Bit **7-27**

File and Branches 7-27

More Practice Entering a Multi-Rung Program 7-30

Unit 8 .... Timers **8-31**

Timer ON-DELAY --(TON)-- 8-32

Timer OFF-DELAY --(TOF)-- 8-34

Retentive Timer RTO 8-37

Self-Test 8-41

Unit 9 .... Counters **9-43**

Count Up Program 9-44

Program using Timers and Counters 9-45

Unit 10 ..... Additional Practice Programs **10-47**

Three Different Flavor Drink Mixer...10-47

Alternate OTE's Energized..10-48

Four OTE's Sequentially Energized Five Times 10-49

Unit 11 ..... Making Voltage Connections to the I/O Modules **11-51**

The I/O Modules..11-51

Safety... 11-52

Unit 12 ..... Connecting External Switches
andField Devices to a Mock Demo Board 12-53

Overview of the Mock Demo Board 12-53

Heater/ Cooler Process 12-54

Creating Subroutine Files and Accessing Them 12-55

Automatic Liquid Recycling System 12-56

Forward/Reversing Moving Activator 12-57

Introduction

This Text/Lab manual is designed to be a programmed learning experience. The instruction begins with an overview of the Allen-Bradley SLC™ 500 Programmable Controller, exploring the module placement and the Hand Held Terminal (HHT). From there the student will learn how to configure the Controller by using programmed instruction for the modules used with the Demo Box supplied by the school. After this task is mastered instructions regarding naming a Program and File are presented, again using programmed instruction. Once these skills have been grasped the student learns how to enter, download, and run a one rung program by following step-by-step instructions. If a mistake has been made, or the program needs to be changed, the student is taken through the steps necessary to modify a rung or individual instruction.

Once the basics are fully understood advanced instructions are presented. The student accomplishes new programming skills by entering and running a multirung program. The use of new instructions are learned by introducing Timers and Counters. Finally three practical industry type applications are added to the text for further practice and application.

UNIT 1

OVERVIEW OF THE SLC™ 5/01 Programmable Controller

The Allen-Bradley SLC™ 5/01 programmable controller is capable of controlling loads, such as motors, relays, or lights depending on input conditions. For example, a switch connected to an input module may determine if a specific output terminal will be activated. A program is written into the programming device and then downloaded to the CPU. When the program is placed in the **RUN** mode the CPU will constantly scan the condition of the input switch specified in the above example. If and when the switch becomes closed the designated output terminal will be activated.

The SLC™ 500 series can be configured in many different ways depending on the application needs. The specifications of the **DEMO UNIT** used at ITT Technical Institute, West Covina, are as follows. **See Figure 1, Following Page.**

Reading Figure 1 from left to right we find:

A 120/240 AC power supply.

In **slot 0** the **5/01**, a CPU with 1K word of user memory. (1747-L511)

Note: If you are using a **5/02** CPU (4K user memory) then select a 1747-L524 when configuring the PLC.

In **slot 1** 4 terminal **Input module.** (1746-1A4)

In **slot 2** 8 terminal **Input module.** (1746-1A8)

In **slot 3** 8 terminal **Output module.** (1746-OA8)

2

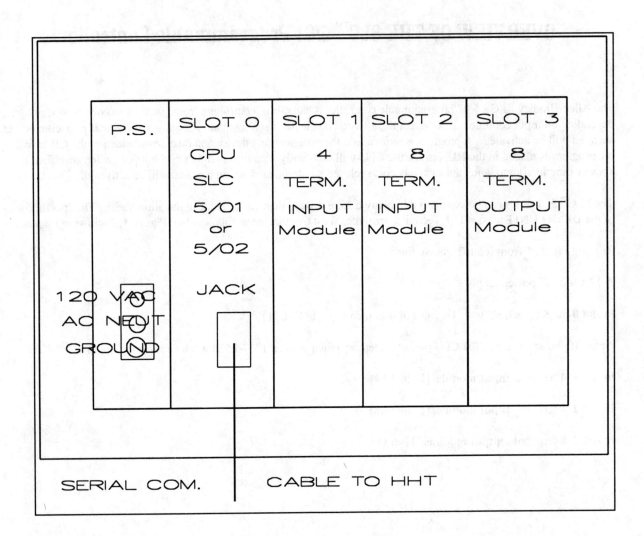

Figure 1: Configuration of the PLC

Demo Box Loads and Switches

Arranged along the lower third of the **demo box** are the loads and switches that are connected to the output and input modules. Notice that there are a total of 8 120 VAC light bulb loads numbered 0 through 7. Six of these loads are combination loads and momentary pushbutton switches; two are loads only, 0 and 7.

Just below the combination loads/switches there are 6 toggle type switches. They are marked 6 through 11. Counting 0 this provides us with a total of 12 input switches, 6 pushbutton and 6 toggle.

See Figures 2,3,4.

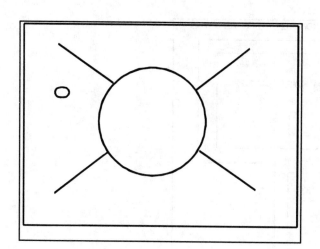

Figure 2: Load only

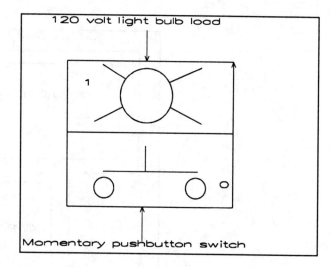

Figure 3: Combination Load and Switch

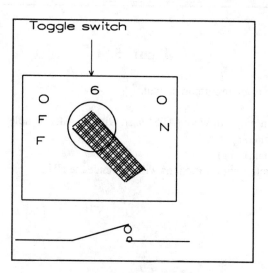

Figure 4: Toggle Switch

The light bulb loads and switches are connected to the output and input modules as follows:

Loads are connected to the **output module (Slot 3)**, terminals 0 through 7.
Momentary pushbutton switches 0 through 3 (4 total) are connected to input module 1 **(Slot 1)**, terminals 0 through 3.
Momentary pushbutton switches 4 and 5 are connected to **input module 2 (Slot 2)**, terminals 0 and 1.
The toggle switches labeled 6 through 11 are all connected to **Input module 2 (slot 2)** terminals 2 through 7 sequentially

The Hand Held Terminal (HHT)

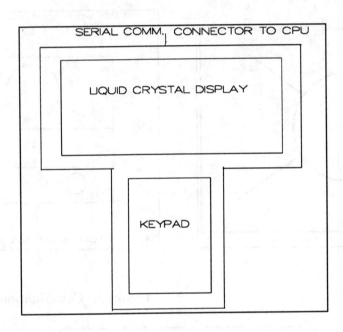

Figure 5.

The SLC™ Programmable Controllers are programmed with:

1) The Advanced Programming Software (APS) used with an Allen-Bradley T50 or T45 terminal or IBM, or IBM comparable personal computer.
2) The Hand Held Terminal (HHT)
In this document all programming instructions will reference the HHT.

Ladder diagram programs or "user programs" are entered into the HHT via the keypad. The instructions written into the program are placed on **rungs** (as in ladder rungs). Typical include (but are not limited to) external **normally open (NO)** and **normally closed (NC)** switch contacts. External Load devices, also known as **field devices,** are designated as **OTE (output energize)**. A sample one rung program is illustrated in Figure 6.

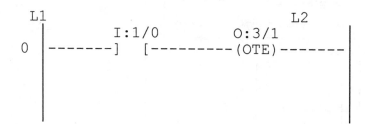

Figure 6.

L1 and L2 represent a 120 VAC bus. Rung 0 of the ladder is connected between L1 and L2. When the **NO** switch contacts addressed as I:1/0 close 120 VAC will be applied to the **OTE** addressed as
O:3/1 and the field device connected to that address will be energized. If it is a light bulb the bulb will light.

A complete discussion of addressing will follow later in the text.

Now that you have familiarized yourself with the layout of the SLC™ 5/01, the demo box, and the HHT, you are ready to follow some programmed instructions.

Preliminary Steps Prior to Applying Power to the Programmable Logic Controller

1. Carefully lift open the small door on the CPU and plug in the smaller of the two ends of the grey cable that connects the CPU to the HHT.
2. Plug the opposite end of the cable into the HHT.
3. Connect the AC line cord to the recessed jack on the demo box.
4. Check to see if all the toggle switches are in the **off** position.

Applying Power to the PLC

1. On the demo box turn the on-off switch to the on position.
2. A red light in the on-off switch should come on.
3. A red LED on the power supply should be on.
4. The CPU fault LED on the CUP should be on briefly then go out.
5. The LCD on the HHT should energize and the HHT should go through a self-test procedure. Once the self-test has been completed the LCD should look like Figure 7.

6

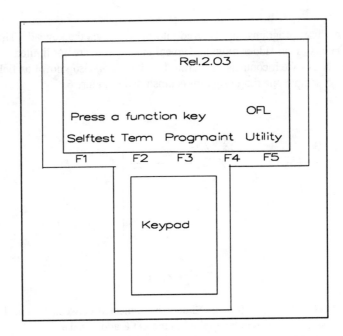

Figure 7.

The designations shown above the **F** keys are for the **main menu** functions. The two we will be concerned with during subsequent lessons are **Utility** and **Progmaint.** Pressing Progmaint (F3) will allow us to work with our program files. Pressing Utility (F5) will enable the sub-menus necessary to connect, or disconnect, the HHT from the CPU.

PRESS F3 NOW

Above the **F** keys the following should be displayed:

CHG_NAM CRT_FIL EDT_FIL DEL_FIL MEM_MAP >

The > at the right side of the LCD tells us that if we press **ENTER** more functions will be displayed.

PRESS ENTER NOW

The following should be displayed:

EDT_DAT SEL_PRO EDT_I/O CLR_MEM   >

Again pressing enter will return us to the previous menu.

CAUTION: Selecting CLR_MEM will delete everything you have entered into the HHT. This includes any programs you may have written. So ask yourself before selecting CLR_MEM, "Do I really want to do this?"

PRESS ENTER NOW

You should have been returned to the PROGMAINT menu the begins with **CHG_NAM (F1).**

Anytime you press the **ESC** key (escape) you will be returned to a higher level menu.

PRESS ESC NOW

You should now have been returned to the **MAIN MENU.**

UNIT 2

Configuring the Controller

While our demo unit has only two input and one output modules, it is possible for the 5/01 to address up to 14 different I/O devices. Because of this versatility the CPU must be told what I/O devices it will be using, and in what slots they are located. This is the purpose of configuration. As previously mentioned, whenever **CLR_MEM** is executed all programs are erased from the HHT. In addition to programs being deleted the configuration is also deleted. Therefore whenever the operator uses the HHT the first thing that must be done is configuration.

IF YOU HAVE NOT ALREADY DONE SO POWER-UP THE 5/01. THE MAIN MENU SHOULD APPEAR.

Controller Configuration Steps

1. Select PROGMAINT (F3)
2. Press ENTER
3. Select SEL_PRO (F2)

Top of screen should read type = 1747-L511 CPU-1K USER MEMORY Series =
Note if you are using a 5/02 CPU, screen should read 1747-L524

4. Press TYPE (F1)

TYPE = at bottom of LCD should be the same as TYPE = at the top of the LCD. If they are equal press ENTER.

5. Press ESC
6. Select EDT_I/O

Notice that the top of the LCD tells us that Rack 1 is a 1746-A4 4-SLOT RACK, and that there is no Rack 2 and 3.
Also the LCD shows Slot 0 = a 1747-L511 CPU.
The center of the LCD shows **Slot 1 = NONE.**

7. Select **MOD_SLT (F2)**

Notice slot 1 = NONE now appears twice.

8. Press the down arrow ∀. Press **ENTER**

Notice Slot 1 now = a 1746-IA4 4-INPUT Module.

9. Press the down arrow ∀ again. Slot 2 = NONE appears.
10. Select **MOD_SEL (F2)**
11. Press the down arrow until 1746-IA8 appears.
12. Press **ENTER**

Notice Slot 2 now = a 1746-IA8 INPUT Module.

13. Press the down arrow ∀ again. Slot 3 = NONE appears.
14. Select **MOD_SEL (F2)**
15. Press down arrow ∀ until 1746-OA8 appears.

Notice Slot 3 now = a 1746-OA8 Output module.

16. Press **ENTER**

If you have completed the above correctly, the controller is now configured properly. Compare the configuration to the configuration illustrated in FIGURE 1.

Press ESC twice. This takes you back to the main menu and ready for the next exercise.

Remember any time you begin programming the 5/01 from scratch you **MUST** re-configure the controller.

Before you go on, complete the **Self-Test on the following page** to insure you thoroughly understand the preceding instructions.

Self-Test

1. How many pushbutton switches are there on the DEMO box?

   6

2. How many output indicator lights are there on the DEMO box?

   8

3. To what module and terminal is light number 3 connected? — OUTPUT

   mod. 3/ term #3

4. To what module and terminal is pushbutton switch number 1 connected? mod 1 / term #1

5. To what module and terminal is toggle switch number 7 connected? mod. 2/ term #3

6. What does **NO** mean? Normally open **NC?** Normally closed

7. What is a Field Device? External load device Give one example. CD Player

8. Unless otherwise stated what is the voltage potential between L1 and L2 of a ladder diagram?

   120 VAc

9. What will happen if **CLR_MEM** is selected? it will Clear the memory

10. Why must the controller be configured every time it is used?
    Someone that used it before might have Programed it different

11. What module must be configured into slot 0? CPU

12. What module must be configured into slot 1? Input module

13. What module must be configured into slot 2? Input module

14. What module must be configured into slot 3? Output module

UNIT 3

Naming the Program and File

In addition to configuring the controller, you must give the program a name before you can begin programming. This Unit shows you how to:

1) Assign a name other than **DEFAULT** to the program.
2) Assign a name to program file 2, the main program file.

If you have not already done so, apply power to the controller and complete the following steps.

1. From the **MAIN MENU** select **PROGMAINT (F3).**
Notice in the upper left-hand corner of the LCD **File Name:**, and **Pros Name: DEFAULT** appears.
2. Select **CHG_NAM (F1)**
3. Select **PROGRAM (F2)**
Notice ENTER NAME: **DEFAULT** appears with a flashing cursor over the **D** in **DEFAULT.**
4. Key in **TEST** and then a space. Notice: When entering letters for a program name you must press **SHIFT** before entering each letter. If you enter numbers only, pressing shift is not necessary.
5. After entering **TEST**, and space, press **ENTER.**
6. Select **FILE (F4)**
Notice **ENTER NAME:** appears with the cursor flashing just past the **:**.
7. Using the same procedure as previous, enter your initials if possible. If the necessary letters are not available use any combination of alphanumeric characters (10 maximum).
8. Press **ENTER.**
Notice **Program Name** is now **TEST**, and File Name is your initials.
9. Press **ESC**

Notice: If at any time you make a mistake while entering the above press **ESC** and begin again.

12

UNIT 4

Memory Organization and Addressing

The processor memory includes Program Files and Data Files. They are organized as shown in Figure 8.

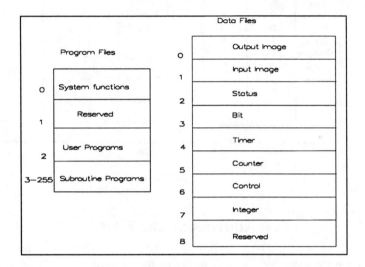

Figure 8.

Program Files

File 0: System functions. Used for a password, identification of a program, and various system-related items.
NOTE: Do not enter any passwords into the training controllers. They must be used by all students and you will not necessarily be using the same one every day.

File 1: This is a reserved file to be used by Allen-Bradley at a later date.

File 2: Contains the user program. All programs you will write will be written into File 2.

Files 3-255 These files can only be accessed from the user program when you use subroutine instructions

Data Files

Data files contain the status information associated with external I/O devices and all other instructions you use in your program. In addition, these files store information concerning processor operation. See Figure 9 for a complete listing of all data file types.

File Type	Identifier	File Number
Output	O	0
Input	I	1
Status	S	2
Bit	B	3
Timer	T	4
Counter	C	5
Control	R	6
Integer	N	7

User—Defined Files		
File Type	Identifier	File Number
Bit	B	
Timer	T	
Counter	C	10—255
Control	R	
Integer	N	

Figure 9.

Addressing the Files

When writing programs into the controller you must designate the addresses of the I/O devices, the bit relays, timers, and counters. Each selected device's address must be in a specific format. The complete address for an **Input** device is shown in Figure 10; the abbreviated version is illustrated in Figure 11.

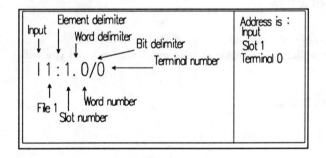

Figure 10., complete Input address

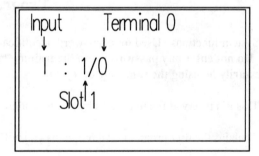

Figure 11., abbreviated address

When you are entering addresses in the ladder diagrams you may use the abbreviated version of the address. The controller will convert these abbreviated forms into complete addresses. The following represents a complete list of I/O addresses, and their abbreviations, used with the SLC™ 5/01 controller as configured in Unit 2.

Input Module (Slot 1)	
Full	**Abbreviated**
I1:1.Ø/Ø	I:1/Ø
I1:1.Ø/1	I:1/1
I1:1.Ø/2	I:1/2
I1:1.Ø/3	I:1/3

Input Module (Slot 2)	
Full	**Abbreviated**
I1:2.Ø/Ø	I:2/Ø
I1:2.Ø/1	I:2/1
I1:2.Ø/2	I:2/2
I1:2.Ø/3	I:2/3
I1:2.Ø/4	I:2/4
I1:2.Ø/5	I:2/5
I1:2.Ø/6	I:2/6
I1:2.Ø/7	I:2/7

Output Module (Slot 3)	
Full	**Abbreviated**
OØ:3.Ø/Ø	O:3/Ø
OØ:3.Ø/1	O:3/1
OØ:3.Ø/2	O:3/2
OØ:3.Ø/3	O:3/3
OØ:3.Ø/4	O:3/4
OØ:3.Ø/5	O:3/5
OØ:3.Ø/6	O:3/6
OØ:3.Ø/7	O:3/7

To reinforce your knowledge of the material presented in the previous Unit take time at this point to do the following **Self-Test.**

16

Self-Test

1. What program file should the programmer use to enter Ladder programs? _____ File 2 _____

2. What is Program File 1 used for? _____ Allen-Bradley _____

_____

3. What Data File is used for the Input Devices? _____ 1 _____

4. What Data File location is used for the Timers? _____ 4 _____

5. What Data File location is used for the Bit Relays? _____ 3 _____

6. What alphanumeric character is used to identify Output devices? _____ O0: _____

_____

7. What alphanumeric character is used to identify Input devices? _____ I 1: _____

8. What is the file number used for timers? _____ 4 _____

9. Write the abbreviated address necessary to identify Input module 1, terminal 3. _____ I: 1/3 _____

10. Write the abbreviated address necessary to identify Input module 2, terminal 6. _____ I: 2/6 _____

11. Write the abbreviated address necessary to identify the Output module, terminal 4. _____ O: 3/4 _____

Now you are ready to begin entering programs into the 5/01 controller.

18

UNIT 5

Entering, Saving and Running a One Rung Program

If you have not already done so, power up your controller. The Main Menu appears on the LCD.

1. If configuration has not been done, do so now.
2. If the Program and File name has not been changed, do so now as outlined in UNIT 3.
3. Select **PROGMAINT (F3)** from the Main Menu.
4. Select **EDT_FIL (F3)**
5. At the **ENTER FILE NUMBER:** Prompt enter **2**
6. Press **ENTER**

You should now see the following on the HHT LCD.

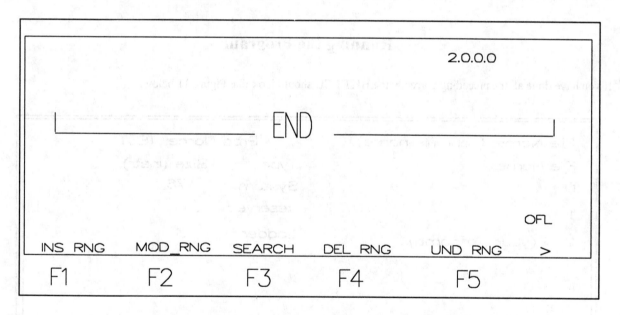

Figure 10.

7. Select **INS_RNG (F1)**
8. Select **INS_INST (F1)**
9. Select **BIT (F1)**
10. Select **NO** contacts -] [- **(F1)**
11. At the prompt **ENTER BIT ADDR:** enter **I:1/Ø**
12. Press **ENTER**
13. Select **ACCEPT (F5)**
14. Select --( )-- **(OTE)** output energize
15. At the prompt **ENTER BIT ADDR:** enter **O:3/Ø**

16. Press **ENTER**
17. Select **ACCEPT (F5)**
18. Press **ESC** twice
20. Select **ACP_RNG (F5)**
You have now successfully written the one rung Ladder Diagram program. Now you will save it.

Saving a Program

Proceeding from step 20 above:

1. Press **ENTER**
Notice **SAVE_CT (F4)** and **SAVE_EX (F5)** appears. If you wished to write more rungs on the ladder you would select **(F4)** then continue adding to the program. In this case you will select **(F5)** which will save your program and exit you from the program writing mode.
2. Select **(F5)** now.
3. Select **ACCEPT (F5)**
A few seconds will elapse while the program is being compiled.
Now you will run your program in the **CPU**.

Running the Program

If you have done all the preceding correctly the HHT LCD should look like Figure 11 below.

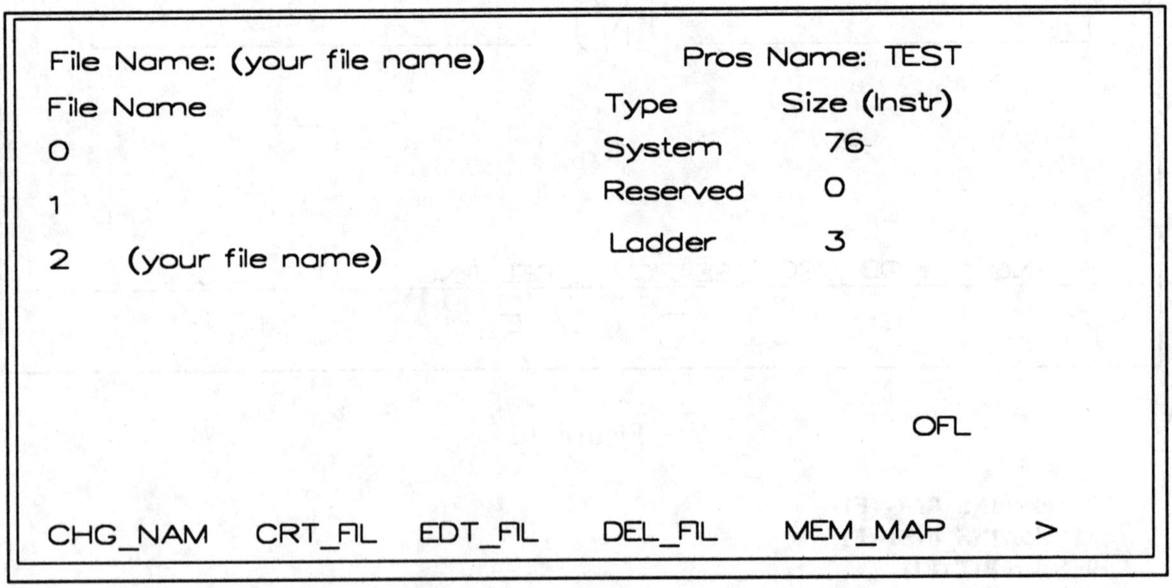

File Name: (your file name)		Pros Name: TEST	
File Name		Type	Size (Instr)
0		System	76
1		Reserved	0
2	(your file name)	Ladder	3
			OFL
CHG_NAM	CRT_FIL EDT_FIL	DEL_FIL MEM_MAP	>

Figure 11.

1. Press **ESC**, this returns you to the **Main Menu.**
2. Select **UTILITY (F5)**
3. Select **ONLINE (F1)** This will connect your HHT to the CPU.
4. Select **ATTACH (F3)**

Note* Attach only appears on this menu the first time you attempt to go online. If you go offline and then back on attach will not appear again.

Note* When you "attach" the top of the LCD must read as follows:

Node Addr.	Device
1	5/01
0	Terminal

Node Addr: 1   Baud Rate: 19200

If, when you attempt to "attach," you get a "Not a Processor" error message ask your Instructor for help.

5. Select **DWNLOAD (F3) (Or F2 if no ATTACH)**
When **"DOWNLOAD TO PROCESSOR?"** appears answer **"Yes" (F2)**
6. When downloading has finished press **ENTER.**
7. Select **MONITOR (F5)**
8. At **ENTER FILE NUMBER:** prompt enter **2** then **ENTER**
You should now see the program you wrote earlier on the LCD.
9. Select **MODE (F1)**
10. Select **RUN (F1)**
11. Answer **"Yes"**

At this time the **RUN light** on the **CPU** should be on, and on the right side of the HHT the LCD should show the word **RUN** flashing off and on.

To activate the light connected to the output module,
terminal Ø, you must depress pushbutton Ø on the DEMO box.

Do so now; light zero should light as long as you keep the pushbutton depressed.

If the light does not light call your Instructor for help.

Note* From now on you should run all your programs in the MONITOR mode.

12. To take the program out of **RUN** mode select **PROGRAM (F5)**.

The flashing **RUN** should change to **PRG** and the run light on the **CPU** go off. Do this now

Clearing the CPU and HHT

At the end of each programming session you will be required to clear both the CPU and HHT before putting it away. To do this effect the following steps:

We will assume you have a program running in the CPU and are in the MONITOR mode.
1. Select **MODE (F1)**
2. Select **PROGRAM (F5)**
3. Press **ESC** twice
4. At the **EXIT MONITOR MODE?** prompt answer **yes.**
5. Press **ENTER** (brings in extended menu)
6. Select **CLR_PRC (F5)**
7. Answer **yes**
8. Press **ESC**
9. At the **CONTINUE AND GO OFFLINE?** prompt answer **yes.**

10. Select **CLR_MEM (F5)**
11. Answer **yes**

Notice the HHT LCD now reads **Prog Name: DEFAULT** and there is no file name. Also the controller configuration and your one rung program has been erased.

Exercise:

1) Return to **UNIT 2** and re-configure the controller.
2) Refer to **UNIT 3** and re-name the program and file.
3) Go to **UNIT 5** and re-enter and run the one-rung program. This time use different I/O addresses. For example you may chose Input module 2, terminal 5, and Output module terminal 3.
4) Clear the CPU and HHT

Repeat the above until you are confident that you can effect all the steps up to this point without benefit of notes. When you feel you have the required confidence move on to the next Unit.

UNIT 6

Modifying a Rung

If, at this point, you have configured the controller, and have given the program and file a name, then proceed with step 1 below. If the HHT is clear then configure, name program and file, and enter the one-rung program from Unit 5, but do not go online and run the program yet.

1. Return to the **MAIN MENU** (press **ESC).**
2. Select **PROGMAINT (F3)**
3. Select **EDT_FIL (F3)**
4. At **ENTER FILE NUMBER** prompt, enter **2**
5. Press **ENTER**

Your one-rung program should now be displayed on the LCD.

If it not call your Instructor for help.

6. Using the right arrow, move the flashing cursor over the normally open **NO --] [--** contacts. Note the address that appears just over the contacts. Address = _I1: 1.0/0_

7. Again, using the right arrow move the cursor over the **OTE**

--( )-- device. Note the address. Address = _O0: 3.0/0_

Now we are going to add a **NC --]/[--** switch contact to the rung. The address will be **I:2/3** which is **toggle switch 7** on the DEMO box. Proceed as follows:

8. Select **MOD_RNG (F2)**
9. Select **INS_INST (F1)**
10. Select **BIT (F1)**
11. Select **NC (F2)**
12. Enter address **I:2/3 ENTER**
13. Press **(F5) ACCEPT**

Your one-rung program should now look like the illustration of Figure 12.

24

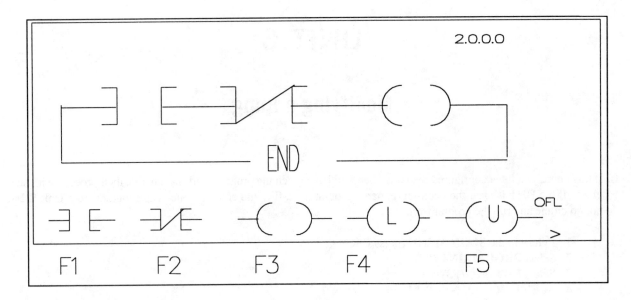

Figure 12.

14. Press **ESC** twice
15. Select **ACP_RNG (F5)**
16. Press **ENTER**
17. Select **SAVE_CT (F4)**
18. Using the right arrow move the cursor to the first contacts **(NO)** on the rung. Above the contacts the address of the contacts should appear (long form).

Record the address:
Long form = I1: 1.0/0
Short form = I: 1/0

19. Move the cursor to the second contact on the rung **(NC)**.

Record the address:
Long form = I1: 2.0/3
Short form = I: 2/3

20. Move the cursor to the **OTE --( )--** on the rung.

Record the address:
Long form = O0: 3.0/0
Short form = O: 3/0

21. Press **ZOOM**. Record in the space below what you observe on the LCD.
Zoom on OTE ( )   2.0.0.0.3
Name: Output Energize
Bit Addr: O0: 3.0/0

22. Move cursor to **NC** contacts. Record LCD readout in space below.
Zoom on XIO ⊣/⊢   2.0.0.0.2
Name: Examine if Open
Bit ADDR: I1: 2.0/3

23. Move cursor to **NO** contacts. Record LCD readout in space below.

Zoom on XIC ⦚⦙⦚   2.0.0.0.1

Name: Examine if Closed

Bit ADDR: I1:1.0/0

24. Select **SAVE_EX (F5)**
25. Select **ACCEPT (F5)**
26. Press **ESC**. You should now be back to the **MAIN MENU**
27. Go online and run your program in the **MONITOR** mode.
28. Activate the switch on the DEMO box connected to the **NO** contacts on the one-rung program. Describe what happens.

The light turns on.

29. Activate the switch connected to **NC** contacts on the one-rung program. Describe what happens.

nothing happens, but if I push the NO switch the light lites up but if I trip the NC switch while pushing the NO the light goes out

Changing Addresses with the ZOOM Control

If you are running the program when you start this topic, take the program out of the **RUN** mode, go offline, and return to the **MAIN MENU. DO NOT CLEAR MEMORY.**

If you are starting from scratch, configure, name program and file, and enter the one-rung program illustrated in Figure 12; then return to the **MAIN MENU.**

1. Select **PROGMAINT (F3)**
2. Select **EDT_FIL**
3. Enter file number **2, ENTER**
4. Select **MOD_RNG (F2)**
5. Select **MOD_INST (F3)**
6. Select **BIT (F1)**
7. Using the right arrow place the cursor over the **NO** contacts.
8. Press **ZOOM**
9. Using the arrows and the keys change the slot and terminal   number. **NOTE*** Slot number can only be 1

or 2, slot number depends on the Input slot you have selected.

10. Once you have made the changes press **ENTER.**

11. Press **ACCEPT (F5)**

The **NO** contacts should now display the new address.

12. Change the address of the **NC** contacts and the **OTE**

by repeating steps 8 through 11.

13. Go **ONLINE** and run the program to see if it performs as   specified.

Making Changes to Rungs

Suppose you discovered you made a mistake on a rung after it had been accepted, or for some reason a **NO** contact must be changed to a **NC** contact. This topic will show you how to make these changes.

If you are running a program, take the program out of the run mode and return to the **MAIN MENU.** If you are starting from scratch, configure, name program and file, and enter the one-rung program illustrated in Figure 12; then return to the **MAIN MENU.**

1. Select **PROGMANIT**
2. Select **EDT_FIL**
3. Enter File Number **2** Press **ENTER**
4. Select **MOD_RNG**
5. Press **ENTER**
6. Move the cursor over the **BIT** you wish to delete.
7. Select **DEL_INST**
8. Answer **YES**
9. Press **ENTER** and **ACP_RNG**
10. Notice the instruction has been deleted.

At this time you could add a new instruction if you wished.

UNIT 7

Entering a Multi-Rung Program
Using the BIT FILE (3) and Branches

In this unit you are going to enter and run the ladder program illustrated in Figure 13.

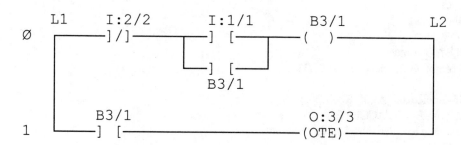

Figure 13.

Two new instructions are shown on **RUNG Ø**. The first is the **BRANCH** instruction, that is in parallel with I:1/1, and the second is the **BIT RELAY** designated **B3/1**. First we will discuss the **BIT** and then the **BRANCH**.

Bit relays are internal logic devices located in File 3; there are 256 of then you can use in your programming. Addressing always starts with **B** (for bit) then a **3** (for file 3) then a / followed by the number of the bit (0-255). When the BIT RELAY on rung one is energized (which will happen when all the rung conditions are true) all contacts with the same address (B3/1 in this case) will activate, if they are normally open they will close, and if the are normally closed they will open.

One set of contacts addressed B3/1 is located in the branch that parallels the pushbutton switch I:1/1. When the pushbutton is depressed the BIT RELAY B3/1 will energize. This will cause the contacts B3/1 across I:1/1 to close **latching** I:1/1. The switch can now be released and relay B3/1 will stay energized.

After answering the following questions you will be ready to enter the program of Figure 13.

    A. Has the controller been properly configured? _Yes_
If the answer is no then configure now following the steps outlined in Unit 2.
    B. Have the program and file names' been entered? _Yes_
If the answer is no change the names now following the procedure outlined in Unit 3.
Entering the program
1. Using the addresses shown in Figure 13, enter the **NC** and **NO** contacts and the **BIT relay** on rung Ø.
2. Once the **BIT ---( )---** has been added press **ESC** twice and accept the rung. You will add the branch after saving the rung. This is so if you make a mistake you can start over by going to **EDT_FIL** and working on the saved program.
3. Press **ENTER**
4. Select **SAVE_CT, ACCEPT**

5. Press **ENTER**
6. Select **MOD_RNG**
7. Select **BRANCH**
8. Move the cursor over the **NO** contacts.
9. Select **INS_BR (F4)**

Notice the small ⋎ is between the **NC** and **NO** contacts; this indicates where the branch will start.

10. The prompt asks you to SELECT BRANCH TARGET. Using the ➤ move the cursor just to the right of the **NO** contacts.
11. Press **ENTER**

The branch has been installed.

NOTE* You can only install one branch at any given location. If you wish to install additional branches on an already existing branch you must use the **EXT_DWN, EXT_UP** instructions.

Now you will install the **NO** contacts on the branch.

12. Press **ESC**
13. Select **INS_INST**
14. Select **BIT**
15. Select the **NO** contacts
16. At the prompt, enter the address **(B3/1)**
17. Accept
18. Press **ESC** twice and **ACP_RNG (F5)**
19. ENTER, SAVE_CT, ACCEPT

You are now ready to enter rung 1 of the program.

20. Press **ENTER**
21. Move the cursor down. The cursor should be flashing on the word **END**.
22. Now starting with the **INS_RNG** instruction, install the **B3/1** contacts and the **OTE**.
23. **ACP_RNG**
24. **SAVE_EX**

You will now analyze your 2 rung program.

Using the **EDT_FIL** option bring your program back on the LCD. Answer the following questions.

1. What type of switch is I:2/2? _NC_
2. What type of switch is I:1/1? _NO_
3. On Rung Ø, what will happen to switch contacts B3/1 (located in the branch) when pushbutton 1 on the demo box is pressed? Explain your answer _The contacts latched_

and light 3 lit up

4. On Rung 1, what will happen to the **NO** contacts (**B3/1**) when pushbutton 1 on the demo box is pressed? Explain your answer.

The contacts latched and light 3 lit up

5. What will be the effect on light 3 on the demo box when Pushbutton 1 is pressed?

it will turn on and stay on

6. Will it be necessary to hold pushbutton 1 down for light 3 to stay on? Explain your answer.

no because it is a latch Circuit

Now following the steps concerning **RUNNING A PROGRAM** in Unit 5, go Online, download and run your program. Press pushbutton 1 on the demo box. Does the program run according the way you predicted it would in the questions you answered above? _Yes_

Operate the toggle switch connected to I:2/2 (actually toggle switch 6 on the demo box) to the **ON** position. Does the light go out? _Yes_

Return to toggle switch to the **OFF** position. Does the light still stay out? _Yes_

Explain why the light did not automatically come back on when the toggle switch was returned to the off position

Because it unlatched the Circuit

With the toggle switch still in the **OFF** position, press pushbutton 1 again. Does the light come back on and stay on?

Yes

More Practice Entering a Multi-rung Program

The program illustrated in Figure 14 is designed to provide you with more practice entering programs with more than one rung. It is also designed to test all the outputs of the output module, and the loads (lights) connected to the output terminals.

Enter, save, and run the program in the **Monitor** mode now.

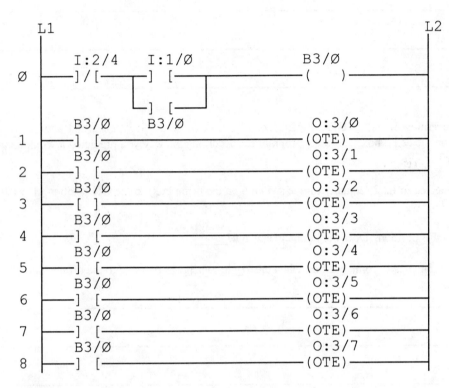

Figure 14.

When you run the above program do all the lights come on when pushbutton Ø on the demo box is pressed? ___Yes___
Do they stay on after pushbutton Ø is released? ___Yes___
When the toggle switch connected to Input Module 2, terminal 4, is turned to the on position, do all the lights extinguish? ___Yes___

If the answers to any of the above questions is **no** carefully examine your program for errors. Go off line and make the necessary corrections, then try it again. If you are still having problems call your Instructor for assistance.

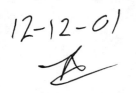

UNIT 8

TIMERS

There are three types of timers you can utilize when programming the SLC™ 5/01 Controller. They are:

  1) Timer **ON-DELAY (TON)**
  2) Timer **OFF-DELAY (TOF)**
  3) Retentive Timer **(RTO)**

These instructions give you many of the capabilities of timing relays. Timer instructions are output instructions you can condition by input instructions such as Examine if Closed and Examine if Open. Figure 15 illustrates a simple example of this. The **NO** contacts on rung Ø addressed as I:1/1 are shown open. If this switch is closed the rung conditions go true and the Timer-On **(TON)** addressed as **T4:Ø** becomes energized and begins counting in 10mS intervals. On rung 1 a switch is shown **NC** but it is in the open position. When it closes the rung conditions become true and the Timer-On addressed as **T4:1** starts counting in 10mS intervals.

```
      L1                                              L2
       |                                              |
       |   I:1/1                       T4:Ø           |
   Ø   |--] [------------------------(TON)------------|
       |   I:1/2                       T4:1           |
   1   |--]/[------------------------(TON)------------|
```

Figure 15.

The Timers-On and the Timers-Off have two values associated with them. They are:

1. Preset value: This is your predetermined set point. This value is entered to govern the timing of the instruction. When the accumulated value is equal to or greater than the preset value timing is complete. The maximum preset value equals **32,767**. Timers count in **10mS** increments; therefore the maximum amount of time a timer can be set to is ≈ 5.46 minutes.

Install Equation Editor and double-click here to view equation.

$$\frac{(32,767) \quad (10 \times 10^{-3})}{60} \approx 5.45 \text{ min.}$$

A preset value of **100** equals **1 second**
A preset value of **1000** equals **10 seconds**
3000 equals **30 seconds**
And **6000** equals **1 minute**

2. Accumulated value: This is the number of units that have been measured for a timer instruction.

To address the Timers begin with the letter **T** followed by a **4** (because the timers are located in Data File 4) the delimiter is a **:**, then the Timer number; this can be any integer from Ø to 255. A complete Timer address is shown in Figure 16.

Figure 16.

Timer ON-DELAY --(TON)--

For Timers to be complete they must have contacts to control. These contacts may be either **NO** or **NC**. These contacts are called **BITS**. The bit numbers may be either **15, 14, or 13.** The function of the three bits are as follows for a **ON-DELAY TIMER** are as follows.

1) **Bit 15** is the enable bit **EN.** When the rung conditions controlling the Timer associated with this bit go true; the bit will set to a **1**.
2) **Bit 14** is the timing bit **TT.** When the rung conditions controlling the Timer associated with this bit go true; the bit will set to a **1** and stay in this condition as long as the Timer is counting. When the preset value equals the accumulated value the timing bit will change to Ø.
3) **BIT 13** is the timer done bit **DN.** When the timer has timed out this bit will set to a **1** and stay in this condition until the Timer is **reset.**

The bits associated with a Timer can be used more than once. For example, if one particular Timer was programmed to control three field devices **(OTE's)** then each one of the rungs controlling the three field devices would have contacts addressed with the Timer number and a **/14** (to control the amount of time the field devices was energized), or a **/13**, to energize the field devices when the Timer had timed-out

To see how Timers works refer to Figure 17.

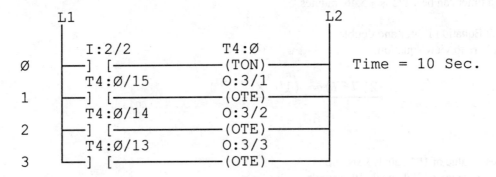

Figure 17.

Here is an analysis of the program shown in Figure 17.

When the toggle switch addressed as I:2/2 is closed the Timer T4:Ø will be enabled. The preset time = 10 seconds. Immediately the **15 BIT** on rung 1 will change to a **1** and the contacts will close which will enable terminal 1 of the output module. Light 1 will light.

Also when the Timer is energized the **14 BIT** on rung 2 will change to a **1** and output number 2 will be energized. Light 2 will light, but will only stay on for the amount of time programmed into the Timer, in this case 10 seconds, then it will go dark.

When the Timer has timed out (10 seconds) the **13 BIT** on rung 3 will change to a **1** and light number 3 will come on. The **13 BIT** and the **15 BIT** will remain a **1** until the Timer is **RESET**, than all bits will return to Ø. This can be accomplished by opening the toggle switch I:2/2.

Using the following instruction sequence, enter the program illustrated in Figure 17 into the HHT. Be sure you have configured the Controller and assigned a name to the program as outlined in Units 2 and 3. When the program has been entered and saved, run the program in the **MONITOR** mode and see if the program performs as specified in the above analysis.

1. Select **PROGMAINT**
[If you have an old program saved in memory select **DEL_FIL**]
2. To begin entering the new program Select **EDT_FIL**, Enter 2
3. Select **INS_RNG**
4. Select **INS_INST, BIT, NO (F1)**, enter bit address **I:2/2**
After accepting the instruction the ➤ appears at the right side of the LCD.
5. Press **ENTER**
6. Select **OTHERS (F5)**
7. Select **TMR/CNT (F2)**
8. Select **TON (F1)**
9. Enter Timer address **(T4:Ø)**
10. Enter **PRESET** time, **1000 = 10 seconds**
11. Enter Ø at the ENTER ACCUM: prompt.
12. Accept
13. Press **ESC** twice and **ACP_RNG**
14. **SAVE_CT**
15. Enter rungs 1,2,3 **(SAVE_CT after each rung to prevent losing the program in the event of a power failure)**
16. After the program has been saved, go **ONLINE, DOWNLOAD,** and run the program in the **MONITOR** mode.
17. Before closing the switch **I:2/2** place the cursor over the Timer on rung Ø and press **ZOOM** Note the status of **EN, TT,** and **DN** before I:2/2 is closed.
EN = ___0___
TT = ___0___
DN = ___0___
17. Now turn **I:2/2** to the **ON** position with the cursor still on **T4:Ø** and **ZOOM** on.
18. Note the status of **EN, TT,** and **DN** while the **ACCUM:** value is increasing to the **PRESET:** value.
EN = ___1___
TT = ___1___
DN = ___0___
18. When the accumulated value equals the preset value note the status of the bits.
EN = ___1___
TT = ___0___
DN = ___1___

34

19. Turn switch **I:2/2** to the **OFF** position. Note the status of PRESET, ACCUM, EN, TT, and DN.

PRESET = 1000
ACCUM = 0
EN = 0
TT = 0
DN = 0

If they are not all **Ø's**, except **PRESET**, check to see if you have done everything correctly. If the program still does not operate according to specifications ask your Instructor for assistance.

Timer OFF-DELAY --(TOF)--

The Timer Off-Delay is similar to the Timer On-Delay as far as addressing, the bit numbers, and entering of the PRESET and ACCUM values. The difference is in the manner the **EN, TT,** and **DN** bits are set. Starting with rung conditions **false,** the sequence is as follows:

Rung conditions false: PRESET = ACCUM
                        EN, TT, DN = Ø

Rung conditions change from false to true: PRESET = preset value
                                            ACCUM = Ø
                                            EN = 1, TT = Ø, DN = 1

Rung conditions change from True to false: PRESET = preset value
ACCUM = counting
EN = Ø, TT = 1, DN = 1

When ACCUM = PRESET EN = Ø, TT = Ø, DN = Ø

Enter the program illustrated in Figure 18 into the HHT, save, go online and run the program in the MONITOR mode. Record the bit conditions as toggle switch **I:2/2** is changed from false to true and then back to false.
Remember to choose **--(TOF)--** rather than --(TON)--, otherwise the procedure is the same as you used to enter the program of Figure 17.

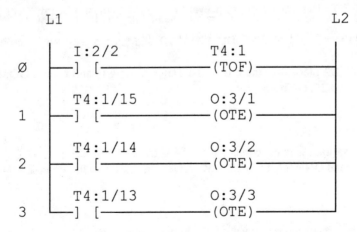

Figure 18.

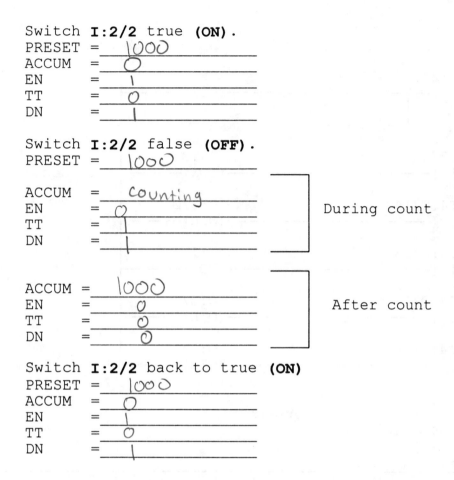

Switch **I:2/2** true **(ON)**.
PRESET = 1000
ACCUM = 0
EN = 1
TT = 0
DN = 1

Switch **I:2/2** false **(OFF)**.
PRESET = 1000

ACCUM = Counting
EN = 0   During count
TT = 1
DN = 1

ACCUM = 1000
EN = 0   After count
TT = 0
DN = 0

Switch **I:2/2** back to true **(ON)**
PRESET = 1000
ACCUM = 0
EN = 1
TT = 0
DN = 1

Figure 19 illustrates a program utilizing both a **TON** and **TOF** Timer. Rung Ø has been programmed with the necessary instructions to control the operation of both Timers. I:2/3 is an emergency stop switch; activating this switch will shut the operation down, I:1/Ø starts the process and is latched by B3/1. B3/1 also activates rung 1; this sets the time operation into motion.

Enter the program into the HHT, save, go online and run the program in the monitor mode. In the space following the program analyze the operation of the program. Specify which lights on the demo box go on, or off, when and why.

36

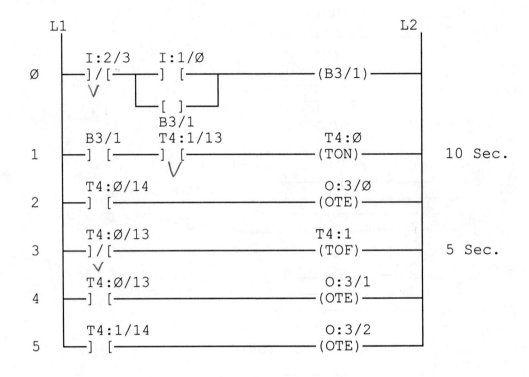

Figure 19.

Your analysis of the Figure 19 program.

From the begining of this Program I Push PB #1
and output #O lights up. After 10 seconds output
#O turns off and output #1 and 2 light up. After
5sec output #1 and 2 turn off and output #O
turns on. This will repeat itself untill switch
#7 is turned to the on position, switch #7 is
I:2/3 which is the reset.

Retentive Timer RTO

Everything you have previously studied regarding the Timer-On, **TON,** is also true of the Retentive Timer, **RTO.** The Bits, **EN, TT,** and **DN** function exactly the same way. The difference between the two Timers is as follows:

When the controlling element on a rung connected to a **TON** changes from **true** to **false** the **TON** will reset the **ACCUM** value back to zero. In addition EN, TT, and DN all are reset to zero.

When the rung conditions controlling an **RTO** change from **true** to **false** the count stops, and the EN, TT, and DN bits reset to zero. When the rung conditions again go true the EN and TT bit are set and the count continues. If the rung conditions stay true the count will continue until the ACCUM value equals the PRESET value. At this time the TT bit resets to Ø, the EN bit stays set (1), and the DN bit goes set (1). If, at this point the rung conditions go false the ACCUM value still equals the PRESET value and EN goes reset (Ø), but the DN bit stays set (1).

To completely reset the **RTO** a reset **(RES)** instruction (usually located on a different rung) must be enabled. When the **RES** instruction is executed the associated **RTO** ACCUM value will reset to zero. When a **RTO** instruction is used in a ladder program a **RES** instruction must also be used. **They both must have the same address.** Figure 20 illustrates an example of this operation.

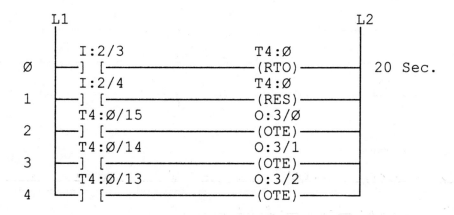

Figure 20.

In Figure 20, when the conditions of rung Ø go true the **RTO** will commence timing in the usual 10mS increments, and EN and TT will set. This will enable OTE Ø and 1. (Two lights will come on.)

If the conditions of rung Ø go false before the ACCUM value equals the PRESET value the timing will stop, and EN and TT will reset to Ø. When ACCUM equals PRESET, EN will remain set, TT goes reset, and DN sets to a 1, OTE 2 is enabled and 1 is disabled. This condition will remain so until the conditions on rung 1 become true activating the **RES** instruction. At this time the **RTO** will reset, and stay reset, as long as the rung conditions of rung Ø remain false.

Following the steps below enter the program of Figure 20 into your HHT.

    1. Using the procedure for entering a switch and a Timer, enter rung Ø. Select **RTO (F3).**

2. Once the rung Ø has been accepted proceed with the following to enter the **RES** instruction.
   a. **INS_RNG**
   b. **INS_INST**
   c. **BIT**
   d. **--] [--**
   e. Enter address I:2/4
   f. Press **ENTER**
   g. Select **(F5) OTHERS**
   h. Press **ENTER**
   i. Select **RES (F1)**
   j. Enter same address as the **RTO**.
   k. **ACP_RNG**
   l. **SAVE_CT**
3. Now using the proper procedures add rungs 2,3,4 to your program.

Once you have saved the program, go online, download, and run your program in the Monitor mode.

1. With the cursor over the **RTO** instruction on rung Ø press the **ZOOM** control.
2. Turn I:2/3 to the on position. (Rung conditions go true.)
3. In the space below record your observations of the Timer conditions.

The accum starts counting En=TT=1 DN=0 after 20sec EN=DN=1, TT=0. Output #0,1 light up, after 20sec Out #1 goes off Out #2 goes on

4. Turn I:2/3 off (Rung conditions go false.)
5. Record your observations.

the ACCUM stops counting but holds its count. EN=TT=DN=0 All lights go out.

6. Turn I:2/3 back to the on position. This time allow the ACCUM value to equal the PRESET value. Record your observations.

Preset=Accum=2000, EN goes from 1 to 0 Output #0 goes off.

7. Turn I:2/3 off again. Record your observations.

EN goes from 1 to 0

8. Turn I:2/4 to the on position. (Rung conditions for the **RES** instruction go true.) Record your observations.

The whole circuit resets ACCUM = EN = TT = DN = 0

40

Timers Self-Test

1. Name the three types of Timers discussed in Unit 7.

   TON   TOF   RTO

2. How much time represents a Timer interval?

   10 ms

3. What is the name given to the two values associated with all Timers?

   -1/2   Preset and Accumulator

4. What is the maximum amount of time that can be entered as PRESET?

   5.45 minutes or 32,767

5. How much time would a PRESET value of 12,000 represent?

   2 min

6. Write the complete address for any Timer.

   T4:0

7. When a **TON** is enabled what will be the condition of the following bits?
   EN = 1
   TT = 1
   DN = 0

8. When the PRESET value equals the ACCUM value of a **TON** what will be the condition of the following bits?
   EN = 1
   TT = 0
   DN = 1

9. What are the rung conditions necessary for a **TOF** to begin timing?   rung logic goes "Lo"
   EN = DN = 1   TT = 0

10. What happens to the ACCUM value of a **RTO** when its rung conditions go false?

    it stops

11. What instruction must be included to reset a **RTO**?   RES

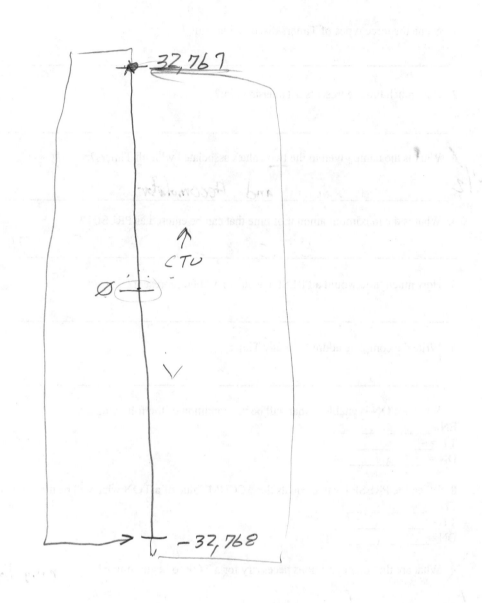

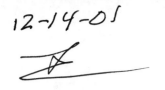

UNIT 9

COUNTERS

Counters can be programmed into the HHT by using either of the following two instructions:

1) Count Up **CTU**
2) Count down **CTD**

Count Up and Count Down instructions count false-to-true rung transitions. These rung transitions could be caused by events occurring in the program such a parts traveling past a detector or actuating a limit switch.

Each count is retained when the rung conditions again become false. The count is retained until a **RES** instruction having the same address as the Counter instruction is enabled.

Each counter has a PRESET and ACCUM value plus a control word.

Data File number 5 is used for Counters therefore the address for counters begins with a **C** for Counter, **5,** Data File 5, followed by a colon. The number after the colon represents the number of the Counter--this may be any number from Ø to 255. The complete address for a Counter could be **C5:Ø**.

The bits associated with a Counter are as follows:
1. Bit 15, **CU** Counter up enable bit.
2. Bit 14, **CD** Counter down enable bit.
3. Bit 13, **DN** Done bit; sets when the accumulated value is greater than or equal to the preset value.
4. Bit 12, **OV** Overflow bit.
5. Bit 11, **UN** Underflow bit.
6. Bit 10, **UA** Update accumulator (High Speed Counters only).

The first program you will enter into the HHT will be a simple one. This program is designed to demonstrate the operation of a **CTU** instruction, Bit 13, and the **RES** instruction. Follow the instructions and enter the program illustrated in Figure 21

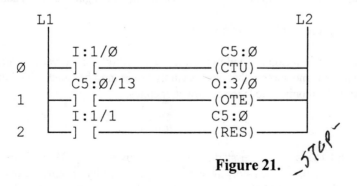

Figure 21.

Entering instructions for Figure 21.

    1. **EDT_FIL**
    2. Enter file number (2)
Rung Ø instructions
    3. **INS_RNG**
    4. **INS_INST**
    5. **BIT**
    6. --] [--
    7. **I:1/Ø**
    8. Enter
    9. **OTHERS**
    10. **TMR/CNT (F2)**
    11. **CTU (F4)**
    12. **C5:Ø**
    13. Enter **PRESET 10** (10 counts)
    14. Enter **ACCUM Ø**
    15. Accept Rung
Enter rung 1 as illustrated
Rung 2 instructions
    1. **INS_RNG**
    2. **INS_INST**
    3. **BIT**
    4. --] [--
    5. **I:1/1**
    6. Enter
    7. Others
    8. **TMR/CNT**
    9. Enter
    10. **RES (F1)**
    11. Accept Rung

SAVE_EX, go online and run your program.

Place the cursor on the **CTU** instruction and press **ZOOM**. Press and release **I:1/Ø** once. Notice the ACCUM value increments once. Press the switch again; the ACCUM value increments again. Continue to press the switch until the ACCUM value equals the PRESET value. Notice that the **DN** bit changes to a 1 and the light at address comes on.

Now press switch **I:1/1**. Notice the counter resets and the light goes out.

The program illustrated in Figure 22 shows how a Counter and two Timers can control a conveyer belt motor and two other motors; one that pushes filled boxes out, and another that pushes empty boxes in to be filled. Read the following analysis then enter and run the program in the monitor mode to see how it operates.

Analysis:

Switch I:2/2 is a **NC** stop switch. Switch I:1/Ø is the master start switch latched by bit relay B3/1; when this switch is pressed the conveyer motor on rung 3 will start. Immediately switch I:1/1, (activated by an infrared detector, whose beam is broken by products passing on the conveyer belt,) begins to make false-to-true transitions. Every time the beam is broken the Counter increments by one. When the count reaches 5 the Counter **DN** bit on rung 3 changes to a 1 and the switch opens disabling the conveyer motor. At the same time the Counter **DN** bit on rung 2 is also enabled and the switch closes enabling Timer T4:Ø. T4:Ø bit 14 on rung 4 changes to a 1 and the **OTE** at address O:3/1 on rung 4 is enabled (this is the motor that pushes the filled box out). T4:Ø times for 15 seconds then the **DN** bit on rung 5 is enabled; this activates Timer T4:1. The 14 bit on rung 6 closes activating the **OTE** at address O:3/2 (this is the motor that pushes an empty box in). When T4:1 times out (15 seconds) the 13 bit on rung 7 closes enabling the **RES** instruction. The Counter is reset and the entire process starts over again, and will continue until the stop button is pressed.

Now enter and run the program and see for yourself how it works.

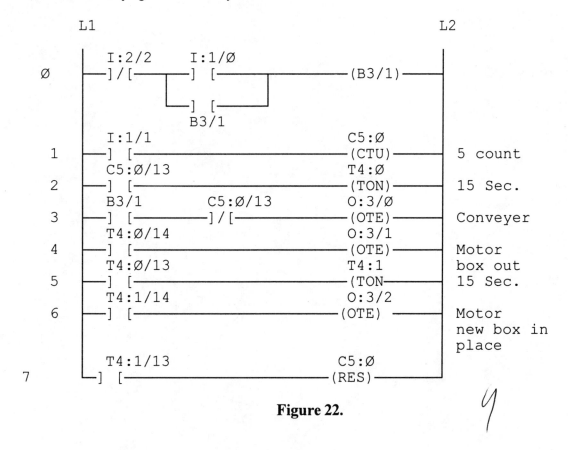

Figure 22.

Figure 4

UNIT 10

Additional Practice Programs

This Unit is included to offer you the opportunity of entering into the Controller additional industry-type programs. Before you attempt entering any of the programming instructions it is strongly suggested you review the basic procedures contained in Units 1,2,3,5.

Program # 1: Three Different Flavor Drink Mixer.

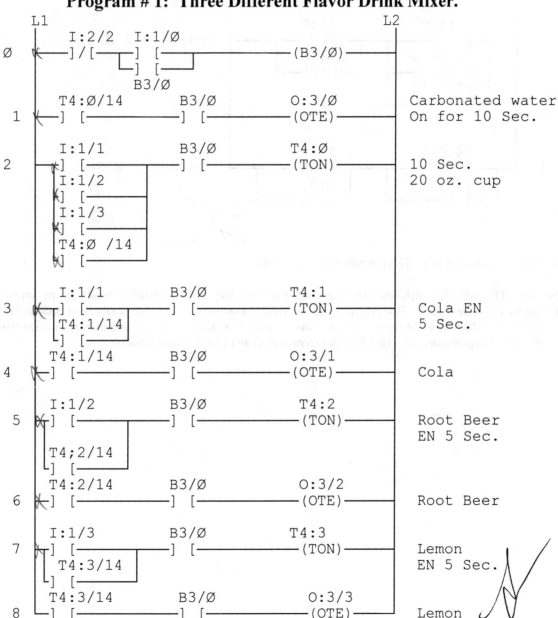

48

Rung Ø of Program #1 is the master control rung. I:2/2 is the system stop switch, and I:1/Ø is the start switch. To activate the entire system the start switch is pressed; this energizes B3/Ø, which in turn activates all rungs. If the stop switch is toggled the entire system is deactivated.

Pressing any one of the three flavor drink switches energizes a flavor Timer for 5 seconds. Pressing any flavor switch also energizes the carbonated water Timer for 10 seconds. To accommodate any mixture ratio the preset of any timer can be changed.

Program #2 Alternate OTE's Energized

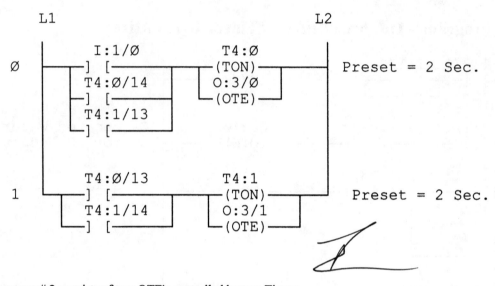

Program # 2 consists of two OTE's controlled by two Timers.

The two OTE's will alternately energize; the amount of time they are on, or off, depends on the amount of time programmed into the Timers. This program could be used to control two lights that would flash back and fourth. Or, using 120 vac relays, it could control two dc motors, each on at alternate times. Another application would be to control two 120-vac motors connected directly to terminals Ø and 1 of the Output module.

Program # 3 Four OTE's Sequentially Energized Five Times

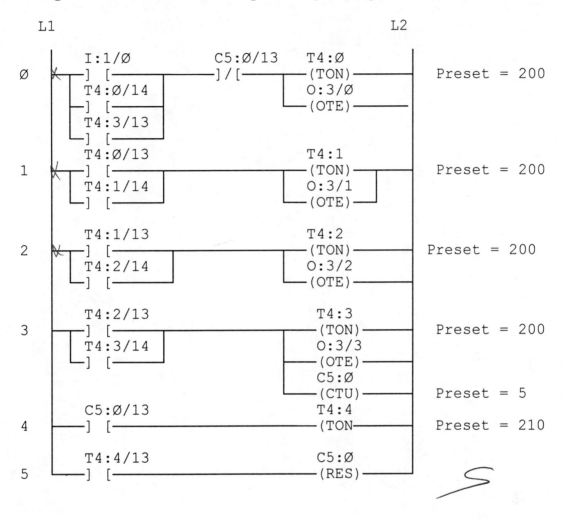

Program # 3 could be used to cycle four different operations sequentially linked. The Counter keeps track of the operations, and at the completion of five cycles the Counter opens contacts **C5:Ø/13** located on rung Ø. This stops the operations until contacts **I:1/Ø** are closed which starts a new 5-count cycle.

50

12-17-01

UNIT 11

Making Voltage Connections to the I/O Modules

The I/O modules used in our labs use 120 VAC. The Input Module requires a 120 VAC input, and the Output Module supplies 120 VAC to external Field Devices. Figure 23 illustrates how the required 120 VAC would be connected to input terminal Ø. Figure 24 shows how to connect an external Field Device, such as a 120 V relay controlling the operation of a motor.

Caution: **Before connecting any external Field Device to an Output Module you must determine the current requirements of the device. The 1746-OA8 output module can supply a maximum of 1.5 amps.**

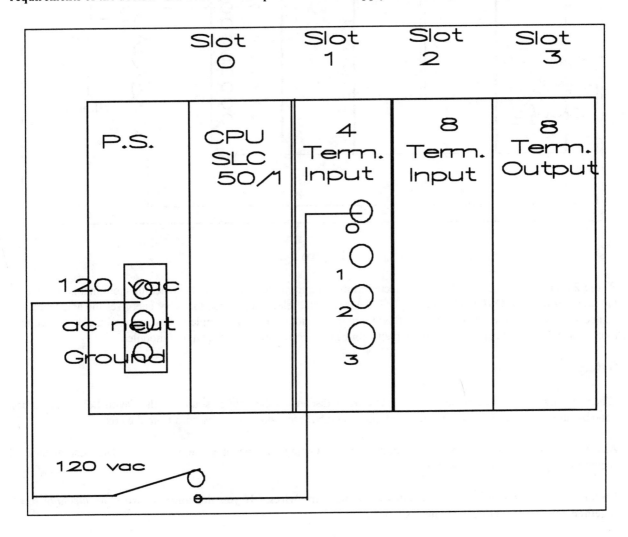

Figure 23.

Notice in Figure 23 one side of a toggle switch has been connected to the 120 VAC terminal on the P.S. The opposite side has been connected to terminal Ø of the Input Module configured in Slot 1. When the switch is closed 120 VAC will be applied to the input terminal **(I:1/Ø)**.

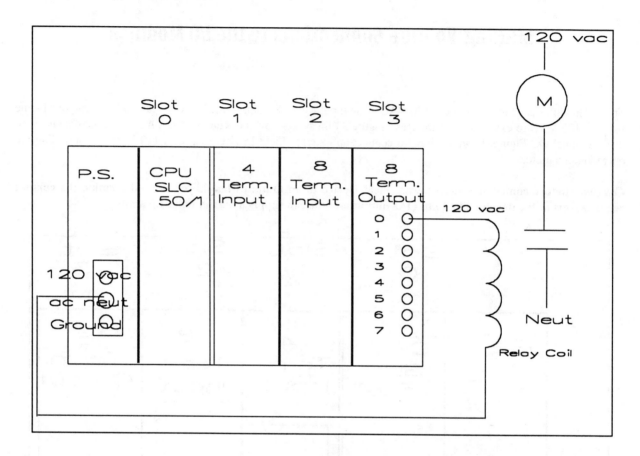

Figure 24.

Figure 24 illustrates a 120 VAC relay connected to the Output module, terminal Ø. When this terminal is selected by the program terminal Ø **(O:3/Ø)** will supply 120 VAC to the relay coil. When the relay energizes the associated **NO** contacts will close allowing ac current to flow through the motor. In this example it was assumed the motor required more than 1.5 amps of current, therefore it could not be connected directly to the Output module.

Safety

When making connections to the I/O modules **always** disconnect the voltage source to the Demo Box. This is best done by turning the On-Off switch to the **OFF** position **AND** removing the power cord from the box.

Any wiring connections to the Input module, or the Output module must be insulated. The best method of accomplishing this is to use **wire nuts.**

Under no circumstances make any splices leaving bare wires. If you do, and the wires *accidentally* touch together, the Output module will be destroyed.

UNIT 12

Connecting External Switches and Field Devices
to a Mock Demo Board
(Advanced Training)

The objective of this Unit is to provide the student with additional experience connecting the PLC to external devices. The devices utilized in this training are: Pushbutton Start and emergency Stop switches, Float (liquid level) switches, limit switches and a solid-state Temperature switch. The Field Devices used are: 120vac Electromechanical Relays, 120vac Reversible Motors, 120vac blower motors, Heaters, Pumps and Solenoids. In addition to the above an On-Off Differential gap controller is integrated into the heat/cool control system. See Figure 25 for a semi-detailed diagram of the complete Mock Demo Board.

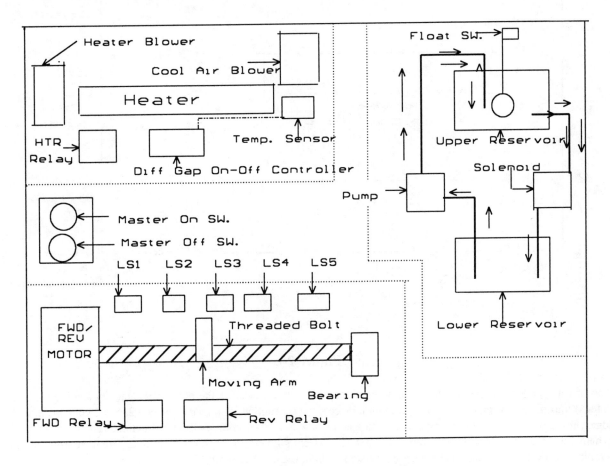

Figure 25.

Figure 25 shows the process control Mock Demo board in three sections.

Heater/Cooler Process

The first is a Heater/Cooler process in the upper left-hand corner of the board. This process consists of a heater controlled by a 120vac relay. After a time delay a blower comes on forcing air along the heater surface to the LM34 temperature sensor. When the temperature reaches approximately 80°F the cooling blower comes-on cooling down the sensor to approximately 70°F. and the cycle repeats itself. The temperature cycling is controlled by a differential gap on-off controller circuit whose input is from the LM34 sensor. The output of the controller consists of a 120vac relay connected to the input module of the PLC. The entire process is controlled by a program entered into the PLC. Figure 26 shows the program followed by a description of the process.

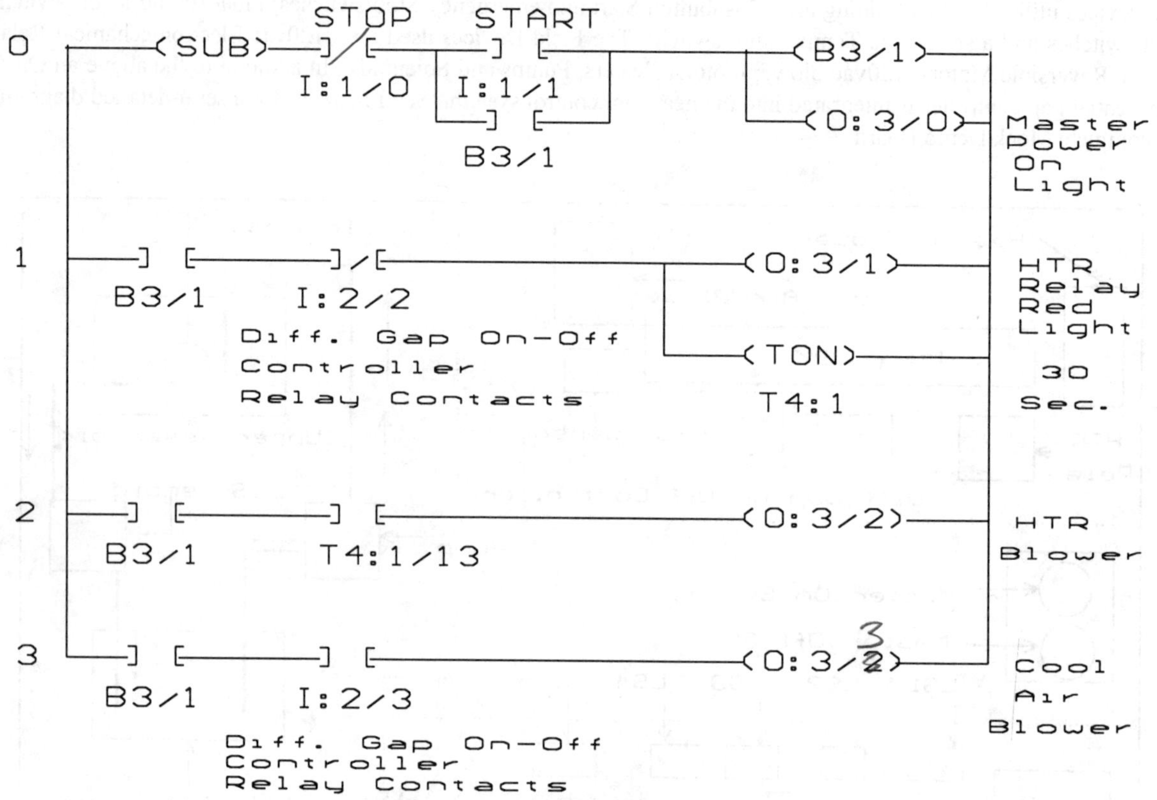

Figure 26.

The first instruction on rung 0 is a (SUB) designation. This is used because the program is actually a subroutine, and entered into file #3 (in this case). The program to access the subroutine is entered into file #2, file 2 contains a ladder logic program containing three rungs, each with a activating switch selecting a (JSR) instruction. The purpose of this scheme is to allow all three programs on the Mock-Demo board to be entered into different subroutine files simultaneously and then selected by the appropriate switch in file #2. See Figure 27.

Notice the STOP switch (I:1/0) and START switch (I:1/1). These addresses are used for the stop/start switches on rung 0 for all three programs on the Mock-Demo board. Also output address (O:3/0) always connects to a green ON indicator light on the Mock-Demo board, again no matter which program is being run. A red OFF indicator light is hard-wired to the OFF switch on the Mock-Demo board. This rung 0 arrangement greatly simplifies the programming of all three programs.

Rung 1 is energized by the contacts B3/1 controlled by the BIT RELAY on rung 0. NC contacts (I:2/2) are the relay contacts connected to the differential-gap controller. Then the relay is energized 120vac will be applied to the contacts causing them to open. When they are closed 120vac will be applied to the heater relay and the delay-on timer. The heater will heat for 30 sec. (or for how much time is programmed in) and then the heater blower will come-on (rung 2) blowing air across the heater to the LM34 sensor. Once the sensor heats to the pre-designated level contacts I:2/3 will close (rung 3) and I:2/2 will open. Cool air will effect the sensor until the state of the differential-gap controller changes causing the relay to again change conditions and the cycle will repeat itself.

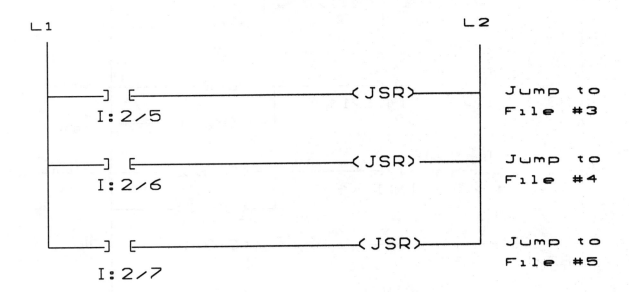

Figure 27.

Creating Subroutine Files and Accessing Them

Begin programming at the program directory.
To create a subroutine file, select CRT FIL
The prompt line will ask for a file number, press 3 and then ENTER.
(Follow the above procedure to create files 4 and 5 for the remaining programs in this unit.)
Select EDT FIL, select file 2 and enter the program shown in figure 27. Closing switch I:2/5 will select file 3, I:2/6   file 4, and I:2/7 file 5.
When the program has been entered into file 2 save and exit.
Edit file 3 and enter the program shown in figure 26.
When the program has been entered into file 3 save and exit.
Go on line and download.
Monitor file 2 and run the program, close switch I:2/5.

While program is running exit from monitor mode and re-select monitor mode, monitor file 3.
Press the master on pushbutton on the Mock-Demo board and the heater circuit should begin to cycle. To stop the process operate the master stop switch.

Automatic Liquid Recycling System

Again referring to figure 25, this time to the upper right-hand section of the Mock-Demo board. Using a pump, a solenoid, two clear plastic tanks, a float switch, and connecting plastic tubing, we have a liquid recycling system. The PLC program to control the process is shown in figure 28 followed by a brief description of its operation.

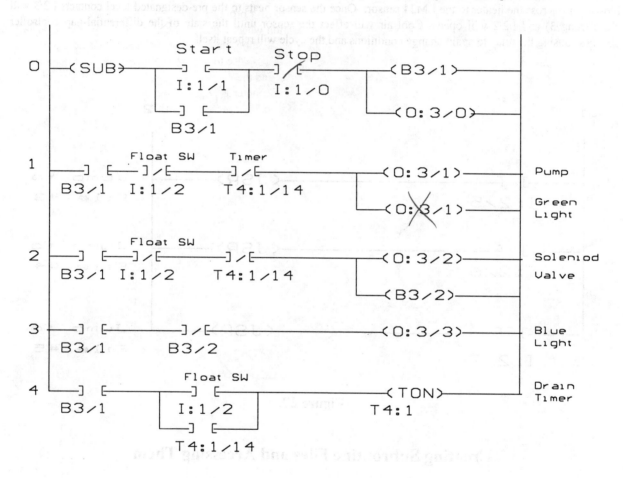

Figure 28.

Rung zero is identical to rung zero of the heater program. Rung one is energized by bit relay B3/1, NC float SW, and NC timer contacts. This will cause the pump to come-on as soon as the start button is depressed. A green indicator light will also illuminate.

Rung two: When the upper container is filled the float SW will close de-energizing the pump and the solenoid. Note: The solenoid used in this case stays closed as long as it is energized and opens when de-energized.

Now the pump is off and the solenoid is open allowing the liquid to drain back down into the lower reservoir until the timer on rung four times-out. Rung three: Blue light is on during drain time.

Rung four: Closed contacts of the float SW, latched by the timer (T4:1) energize the timer preventing the pump and the solenoid from changing states during drain time. Time entered into the timer will depend on the storage capacity of the liquid containers. Once the timer times-out the entire process will repeat itself and will continue to do so until the stop switch is activated.

Forward/Reversing Moving Activator

The third demonstration on the Mock-Demo board is a simulation of a process involving a moving arm the activates different limit switches as it travels. The process could be a situation where a part moves through the process and each time a limit switch is activated some event effects the part such as cleaning, painting, drying etc. In this case a counter in incorporated into the PLC program. Each time a limit switch closes (false to true) the counter counts up one. When the count reaches four the forward motor control relay de-energizes and the reverse relay energizes causing the motor to reverse direction. When the moving arm contacts limit switch 1 the counter is reset and the entire process begins again. Figure 29 shows a detailed drawing of the hardware involved, figure 30 shows the motor and relay wiring, and figure 31 the program itself.

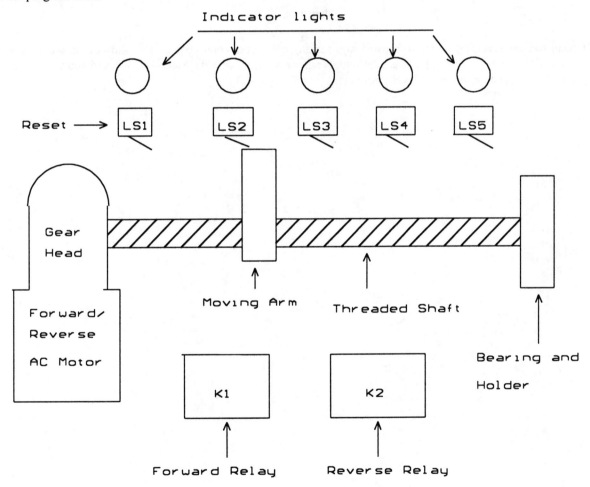

Figure 29.

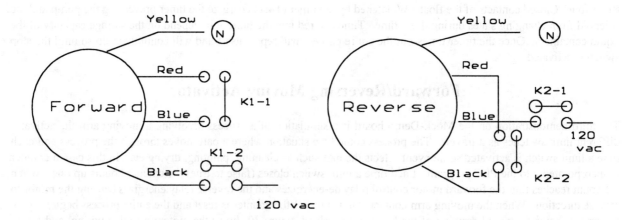

Figure 30.

A typical forward/reversing motor with two relays making the proper connections. This shows only one of several possibilities and may or may not represent the actual connections used with the Mock-Demo board you will be using. If you have any questions check with your instructor.

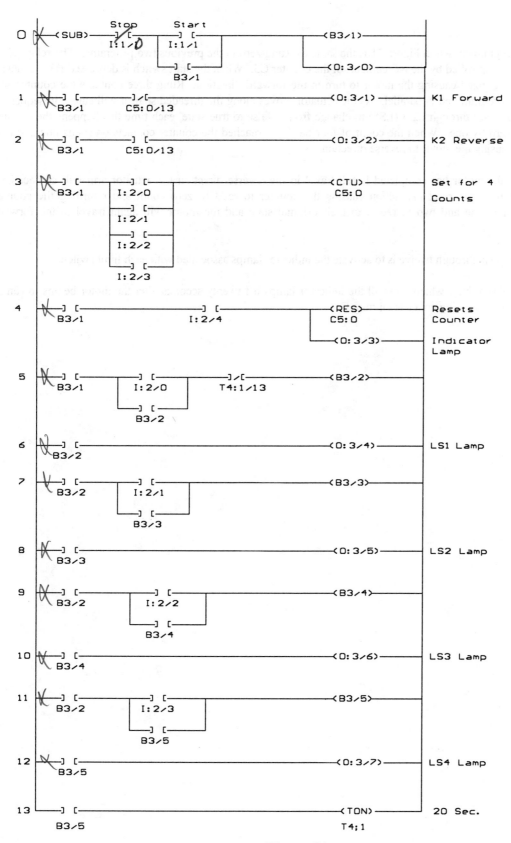

Figure 31.

Rung zero of the program shown in Figure 31 is the same as Rung zero in the previous two programs. The relay (K1), shown in rung one is controlled by the NC contacts of the counter C5. When the start switch is depressed B3/1 contacts go true and K1 is energized causing the motor to turn in the forward direction. Rung three contains the counter and four input switches programmed in parallel. As the actuator moves along the threaded shaft it will cause, in sequence, limit switches I:2/0 (LS2) through I:2/3 (LS5) to change from a false to true state, each time this happens the counter will increment upward by one. When the count of four has been reached the counter contacts on rungs one and two will change states causing the motor to reverse direction.

Rung four: When the motor has completed is full travel in the reverse direction the actuator arm will contact LS1 (I:2/4) this will activate the reset instruction causing the counter to reset to zero count and returning the counter switches /13 on rungs one and two to return to their original state and the motor will again travel in the forward direction.

The purpose of rungs six through twelve is to activate the indicator lamps associated with each limit switch.

Rung thirteen contains a timer which turns all the indicator lamps off twenty seconds after the motor begins to run in the reverse direction, controlling contacts on rung five.